The design of veteran cars like this 1902 James and Browne offered no protection from the elements. These lady passengers, perched up high, are wearing fur stoles, small hats with gauze veils and a leather wrap for the legs. The driver wears a single-breasted woollen coat with astrakhan collar.

MOTORING COSTUME

Andrew Lane

Shire Publications Ltd

CONTENTS

Set in 9 point Times roman and printed in Great Britain by C. I. Thomas & Sons (Haverfordwest) Ltd, Press Buildings, Merlins Bridge, Haverfordwest, Dyfed.

British Library Cataloguing in Publication Data available.

Editorial Consultant: Michael E. Ware, Curator of the National Motor Museum, Beaulieu.

ACKNOWLEDGEMENTS
All the illustrations used in this book come from the Photographic Library of the National Motor Museum, Beaulieu, Hampshire.

COVER: *Warm overcoats were essential for riding in open cars in Edwardian times, and ladies' hats had to be securely fastened down with yards of gauze veil.*

LEFT: *During the Edwardian era many leading stores like Dunhills, Aquascutum, Gamages and Burberrys produced special clothes for motorists. The model in this advertisement has all the necessary items for summer motoring: dust coat, gloves, goggles and hat with a gauze or chiffon veil.*

In 1900 roads were basically dirt tracks made of stone. As cars, like this De Dion, became capable of greater speeds, dust was thrown up from the dry surface in summer. The motorists' only recourse was to dress up in protective clothing to keep the dust out of their eyes, hair and finer undergarments.

INTRODUCTION

The motorists of today do not give a second thought to driving in their ordinary, everyday clothes. It is the natural thing to do. If the driver feels cold he or she can switch on the heater, or the air conditioning can give a steady flow of cool fresh air when it is too hot. The modern driver, cocooned within a car body of steel and glass, can control his environment. To the Edwardian motorist such an idea would have been pure science fiction.

To these pioneers dressing for a car journey was all part of the motoring experience, along with punctures and breakdowns. To understand why they needed special motoring clothes, it is necessary to look briefly at the development of car design. During the 1890s the motor car resembled an elegant horseless carriage, capable only of very low speeds. Such vehicles, driven by chauffeurs, could be seen around the parks of London and Paris during the weekends. The occupants' clothes were no different to those worn for travelling by horse-drawn carriage.

By 1900 the car had developed so rapidly that speeds of 50 mph (80 km/h) could now be attained. This brought new problems for the motorist. Motor cars were of an open design and most had no windscreen, roof or doors. The occupants sat up high, completely exposed to the wind and weather. The increased speed of cars also threw up dust from the roads, which were simply made of compacted stone. In summer this dust contained the dried remains of horse manure, for road transport was still dominated by the

ABOVE: *This rare scene of a car in motion with a dust storm in its wake illustrates clearly how serious the dust problem was. It was far worse for people in another car following behind or even for other road users.*

BELOW: *Some motorists had no regard for how they looked. In this scene in France in 1905 there are a variety of goggles and styles of clothing. The driver is wearing breeches with leather leggings. The lady's headwear is made from wool with a woven pattern and securely fitted around the face and neck.*

horse. Therefore if a motorist wanted to keep dry, warm and clean he had to dress in protective clothing. During the period 1900-12 a new line in fashion evolved for motorists. Since cars were extremely expensive during this period, only the wealthy could afford the luxury of motoring and they turned to their London tailors and milliners for their motoring needs. Dunhills, Aquascutum, Burberrys, Gamages and Harrods were some of the leading London stores which created new lines of motoring clothing. The lady motorist or passenger could spend up to £300 for a complete wardrobe of fashionable garments to cope with winter and summer motoring, an enormous sum when compared to the wages paid to her maid of about £60 a year.

Like any other kind of clothing for wealthy clients, motoring costume was continually changing to the whims of fashion. Ladies' magazines and motoring journals published regular articles on what was new and chic for the coming season. Hats were particularly liable to changes in style and fashion.

However, as car design improved to give greater weather protection, the need for specialised motoring clothing decreased. By the 1920s the all-enclosed saloon had become increasingly commonplace and only the sports car driver continued using goggles and caps. However, drivers of saloon cars still needed warm clothing in winter for several more decades. The car heater did not become a standard feature until the 1950s. By the 1920s roads had also improved enormously with the use of tarmacadam. The days of dust and exposure to the elements were over.

With the chauffeur in the back seat, the owner of this 1902 16 horsepower De Dietrich wears a coat of wolf fur. Fur coats had the disadvantage of holding dust and dirt and became unpleasant when wet. Note the muddy road conditions.

Winter motoring outfits for ladies and their chauffeur about 1903. He is wearing a leather jacket, breeches and leggings. The lady in the light-coloured woollen coat would find the wide open cuffs very draughty. The dark fur coat is possibly foal skin, which became quite popular. The car is a 15 horsepower Panhard.

COATS

From 1896, when the motor car first appeared in Britain, until about 1903 drivers tended to wear rough coats because of the frequency of breakdown, which required the driver to get out and underneath the car. For doing this or even tinkering under the bonnet drivers wore utility coats or jackets with little regard for fashion. However, the reliability of cars improved rapidly and the need for roadside repairs became less frequent. Motorists took greater care over their appearance but coats still had to be functional.

These requirements were a challenge to the designer of motoring coats. The coat had to keep out chilly winds; it needed to be waterproof; collars when raised must exclude draughts; the gar-

ment should cover the knees and thighs when the driver was seated but had to have neatness with style. The ladies' Edwardian overcoat, whether it was a summer dust coat or heavy tweed for winter, was cut to a bodice figure and opened out to a full skirt. The men's coat was fuller and not so close-fitting. Coats for both sexes were buttoned double-breasted, which gave a double layer of thickness for warmth. Collars were deep and capable of being turned up above the ears. The cuffs were closed against the wind by using straps either hidden behind folds or integrated into the design.

In winter most car owners stored their cars away, since motoring was considered by many as a summer pastime rather like sailing or fishing. For the hardier motorist a fur coat seemed an obvious choice. The continental fashion was for fur coats with the fur on the outside but this style was never very popular in Britain. Burberrys' catalogue stated: 'English gentlemen do not take kindly to the Continental monstrosities in the shape of horseskin, sheepskin, wolfskin and variations of coats which have the hair, wool and fur outside. The more distinguished form is to use the fur simply as a lining. The outside presenting the appearance of ordinary travelling Ulsters.' However, the British motorist still looked on France as the world's leading motoring nation and so some followed the continental tradition of fur coats. In 1902 Dunhills offered a white seal coat with opossum collars. Seal was a very serviceable material for the motorist since it could be washed with soap and water and always maintained a fresh, smart appearance. An altogether more substantial garment was the vast coat of Australian fox or Siberian wolf. One of the most expensive coats for men was the 'Club' coat of beaver lined with mink, costing £63.

For ladies full fur coats were far more acceptable. The variety of furs available was enormous and many were rare and exotic. One firm offered a coat of silver baboon with the collars and revers made of lynx. Another exclusive outfit was a long coat of wildcat skin with a collar of racoon. In 1902 Dunhills offered a voluminous fur cloak of lynx or opossum lined with satin and completed with a squirrel hood. Other kinds of fur commonly used were marmot, opossum, beaver, squirrel, musquash (musk rat) and chinchilla.

Most British motorists did not favour coats with fur on the outside, although they were popular on the continent, but Lord Northcliffe in this huge bearskin was an exception.

"KERRY" WEAR FOR MOTORISTS.

Wonderful Value in

FUR LINED COATS.

IRISH FRIEZE, FUR LINED.

These Ulsters are supplied in a variety of patterns of Irish Frieze Cloths, **lined with warm Fur.** A most comfortable and cosy garment for motoring, and wonderful value.

			Each.
No. MC500	Frieze, Lined Hamster		£5 17 9
No. MC501	,, ,,	Electric Rabbit	£6 15 0
No. MC502	,,	Marmot (whole skins)	£9 9 0
No. MC503	,,	Marmot (pieced skins)	£6 0 0
No. MC504	,, ,,	Dyed Wallaby	£9 0 0
No. MC505	,, ,,	Musquash	£12 0 0

BLACK BEAVER, FUR LINED with FUR COLLARS.

		Each.
No. MC510	Beaver, lined black electric rabbit with electric collar ...	£15 0 0
No. MC511	Beaver, lined Marmot with nutria Beaver collar ...	£15 0 0
No. MC512	Beaver, lined rabbit with Persian Lamb collar ...	£15 0 0
No. MC513	Beaver, lined Musquash with Persian Lamb **long roll collar**	£21 0 0

		Each.
No. MC506	West of England Cloth, lined Musquash	£15 0 0
No. MC507	Irish Cheviot, lined Musquash...	£12 0 0

Fine coats for English gentlemen with the fur on the inside. The choice of fur for the lining was extremely varied, ranging from hamster to wallaby. The Ulster coat was a popular and traditional travelling coat.

Winter driving in a car such as this 16 horsepower Decauville must have been cold and miserable. However, these occupants are clearly showing that motoring outfits do not need to be outlandish or peculiar to motoring. The driver's overcoat has a beaver collar with leather cuffs.

Fur-lined coats of the English style for both men and women were usually made of Scottish tweed or Irish frieze and were double-breasted with fur on the collars. These wool and fur coats were very heavy and bulky and must have been very tiring to wear for any length of time. For instance the Burberry 'Viator' weighed 12½ pounds (5.67 kg).

The motor car was responsible for the encouragement of the use of leather in clothing. Before 1900 leather was being used for hems, pipings, collars and cuffs but it was then discovered that it was the ideal windproof material. A fashion writer at the 1904 Motor Exhibition was impressed by a coat of myrtle-green leather, cut double-breasted and three-quarter length. There were slender leaf-like revers, a storm collar and cuffs of green cloth embroidered in green and gold coloured silks, and decorating the front were two rows of brass buttons with centres of embroidery.

Leather coats were made available in a variety of colours: for the 1907 season, for example, Drykitt of Oxford Street offered coats of plain blue, green, violet and grey. The most common use of leather, however, was for detachable coat linings. The winter cloth coats and even some summer dust coats frequently had leather linings. Another variation was a coat with a lining covering just the bodice section. Chamois leather was recommended as the best lining because of its softness and lightness.

Despite the windproof qualities of leather and its obvious advantages for open-air motoring, it had one serious disadvantage: being airproof, leather gave no ventilation to the body and became unhygienic. Baron De Zuylen De Nyevelt, President of the French Automobile Club, wrote in an article on motoring clothes in 1902: 'A leather jacket and leather trousers are objectionable because the moisture from the body

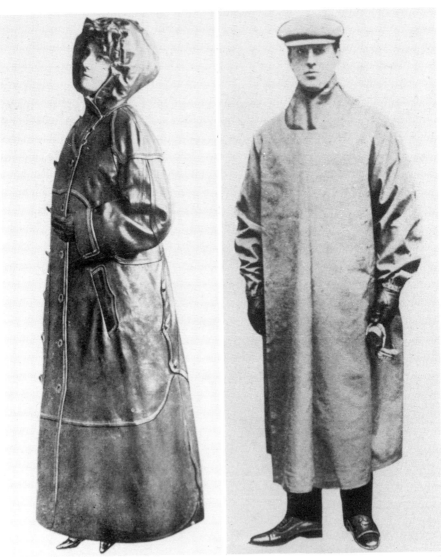

LEFT: *A green leather coat with a hood that could be tightly drawn around the face with a silk cord and buttoned under the throat to protect the hair. The yoke is drawn in at the back with a small strap and the whole coat allowed plenty of fullness in the skirt when seated.*

RIGHT: *The 'umbrella' coat was the ultimate stormproof protection. It had a tightly fitted neck of elasticated rubber, through which the wearer pushed his head. It was made in either waterproof twill or a rubber-proofed material.*

LEFT: *The 'Kennard' mackintosh was designed by a leading lady driver in 1910. It buttoned at the side under the left arm leaving no seams exposed to the force of the rain. The additional yoke gave double protection on the chest. The coat was made from waterproof twill, silk or mackintosh silk.*

RIGHT: *This storm coat has drawstrings at the neck and elasticated wrists. One of the hazards of these coats was that the wind blowing up inside made them difficult to drive in.*

LEFT: *A double-breasted Harris tweed coat with fancy strappings of faced cloth and lined with silk. This coat cost £11 11s in 1910.*

BELOW: *This hood incorporates a mica veil for eye protection and lace covering the lower face. The silk hood fitted over a straw hat and protected the ears and neck from draughts. The magnificent tweed coat has kimono sleeves, and body and sleeves are lined with silk. The unusally high, shaped collar gave excellent protection and warmth.*

cannot escape, with the result that under-clothing becomes dangerously moist and disagreeable.'

Apart from the cold, the driver had to protect himself from rain, especially if he was motoring in Britain. What a miserable experience it must have been to drive at speed, perched high up on a vehicle that offered no protection what-ever. 'For wet weather there is nothing better, in my opinion, than the rubber-necked umbrella mackintosh smocks, with a light yachtsman's sou-wester as head covering,' wrote an *Autocar* columnist in 1904. Dunhills were selling the umbrella coat from 1902 and their advertisement tried to describe it: 'It is to all intents and purposes a loose, long cape with sleeves, made of the best rubber spread on the usual fabric, but the neck consists of rubber alone, so that there is no button on the garment and the head is pushed through the elastic orifice.' A case was supplied with each coat for its storage.

The most popular raincoats for men were those made from gabardine and aquascutum. They were waterproof, light and well ventilated and so were ideally suited for motoring. One style of Burberry gaberdine coat had a distinctive puttee collar. The coat met in front, with the left side folding over and an extended piece wound around the neck in puttee form, enclasped at the back on a stud clip. This effectively kept out water or dust yet gave a neat appearance. The other very popular and versatile Burberry coat was the waterproof slip-on. Aquascutum was, like gabardine, an ideal material for motoring coats, being made of wool and waterproofed. Messrs Aquascutum of Regent Street gained enormous prestige by supplying coats of their special material to King Edward VII and the Prince of Wales. By 1909 the range of Aquascutum coats included three different styles for men, while for the ladies three different weights of coats were available to suit summer or winter motoring. Many other companies provided proofed coats, mainly in Irish frieze and Scottish tweed for colder weather, and most motorists preferred to use proofed coats rather than leather or furs.

To the Edwardian motorist summer brought road dust. It was a problem that was overwhelming and the only answer

A 1904 summer motoring coat in white homespun with winged cuffs that could be fastened across the wrist with a strap. It is a double-breasted coat which could be turned back on either side and buttoned down. The coat is given shape at the back by a gathered waist and held by two bands.

CHIC
MOTORING
ATTIRE
AND
EQUIPMENT
AT
DUNHILL'S,
NUMBERS
TWO ∾∾∾

AND FIVE,
CONDUIT STREET,
REGENT STREET, LONDON W.

OPPOSITE: *It is hard to believe that this advertisement appeared in the 'Car Illustrated' magazine in 1904. The skirt, for example, is very short for the period. This fashionable look would not be out of place in the 1970s or 1980s, with the exception of the goggles. A yachting or military peaked cap, leather jacket and knee-length lace-up motoring boots have no parallels in other Edwardian motoring outfits.*

RIGHT: *Children's outfits were usually tailor-made in styles similar to those worn by adults. This girl's summer outfit would be lined with fur or fleece and the loose-fitting straw hat and veil would not crush the hair.*

was to wear protective clothing. The summer dust coat became the most stylised item in the motoring wardrobe. The coat had to be a compromise between elegance and practicability. Ladies' dust coats were outstandingly successful in this respect. The most sensible and popular colours for coats were dust shades, namely beige, grey, cream and fawn. The variety of fabrics used for dust coats was considerable and each could be selected on its merits of warmth, lightness, dust-repellent quality or smartness of appearance. Tweed, alpaca, holland, twill, worsted, crash, serge, Shantung and Tussore silks, gabardine and mohair were all available in a variety of styles. The finest dust coats were made of silk, which was a naturally good dust repellent, light, very soft and hard-wearing and allowing a graceful flow in the skirt. Men's as well as women's coats were available in silk and sold for about £3 3s. Serge was favoured by some because it did not crease like silk, linen or alpaca.

Another problem of summer motoring in Britain was the unpredictability of the weather, so apart from the cool and attractive silk coat motorists also bought rainproof linen, gabardine or the warmer alpaca or tweed coat. Deciding what to wear for a Sunday drive was always a dilemma for the Edwardian motorist.

CHILDREN'S CLOTHES

Motoring outfits for boys and girls were very similar to the adult selection. The 1908 catalogue of Hyams of Oxford Street contained a large selection for children. For girls there were white rabbit coats with a white satin lining at £3 13s 6d or the very soft goatskin coats with checked lining and grey pebble buttons. For teenage girls, a tan leather coat had a storm collar and wind sleeves with an outside strap. Other winter items of pony skin or dyed musquash were very expensive at £7 7s and £10 10s respectively. More often tailors and retail stores did not specify their range of children's clothes but offered made-to-measure outfits allowing for individual choice of style and materials.

ABOVE: *Some hideous examples of headwear worn by ladies around 1900. (Left) Tinted glasses set in a silk mask, which was still available up to 1912. (Centre) A full face mask of silk with nosepiece but with no apparent ventilation for the mouth. (Right) A crêpe-de-chine hood with goggles. It kept the hat secured but at what price!*

Harrods

Charming Motor Millinery.

Carriage paid in United Kingdom.

Orders by post carefully executed.

No. 4012.

No. 4001.
Charming Fur **Toque**, in grey Squirrel.
Price **55/**
Very suitable for smart wear, with an osprey, ostrich feather, or coque mount added.

No. 4009. Useful Fur **Toque**. The crown is of electric seal, with an effective brim of opossum. Light and good fitting.
Price **59/6**
Can be made in any fur. Price according to quality used.

No. 4009.

No. 4016.

No. 4012. Soft and comfortable **Motor Hood** of electric seal.
Price **2 gns.**
Can be procured in other furs if desired. Prices according to skins used.

No. 4016. Motor **Toque** fitting tightly round the hair. The crown is of plain silk bordered with Paisley, with small pleating coming from under, making the Toque soft and becoming. In all new shades.
Price **2½ gns.**

HARRODS L^{TD} RICHARD BURBIDGE, MANAGING DIRECTOR. Brompton R^d. London S W

LEFT: *This advertisement dates from 1912 and reflects the growing fashion for toques, which were much more practical for motoring than the usual wide-brimmed Edwardian hat secured by a veil. The prices quoted are about average for a fur hat of the period.*

CAPS, HELMETS, Etc.*

The "Arctic" Fleecy Wool Cap.

Can be worn in three positions—

1. Turban Style. 2. Turban with Peak (as illustrated).
3. "Pullover," gives complete protection to neck and ears (as illustrated).

		Each
No. MC290.	Heather Mixture shades	2/3
No. MC291.	Super quality, with wind resisting sateen head lining, all shades	3/3
No. MC292.	Plain Turban shape (without face opening)	2/-

The "Varsity" Racing Helmet

in Brown or Black Leather with Ear
rolls for wind protection.

		Each
No. MC293.	Sateen lined ...	9/9
No. MC294.	Fleece lined ...	10/6

The "Peary."

No. MC167. Stocked in a large variety of
patterns in all sizes. The strap can be
brought down under the chin, and back
dropped over the neck, each, 2/6.

Showing Goggles when not in use.   Goggles in use.

The "Motorbike."

No. MC170. This cap is made of rainproof material and is fitted with goggles on one
side and peak at the other. By a simple adjustment both goggles and peak can be worn
turned up or down as required.   Each 7/6.

Golf Shape Caps.
No. MC171.
Stocked in a variety of shades and all sizes, each, 2/6

"The Mask."
No. MC169.
Fitted with goggles which can be
brought down over the eyes or
turned back as required.
Each 7/6.

The "Shackleton."
No. MC168. The leather band to this cap is
semi-detachable, enabling a **fur-lined flap to
be pulled down** (as illustrated) giving warmth
and full protection to the neck and ears, each, 5/-

WATERPROOF CAPS
to match our Motor Cycle Suits.
No. MC172. Each 5/-

*When ordering Caps please state size required.

*The 'Peary' represents one of the commonest choices for a man's motoring cap. The 'Motor Bike'
and 'Mask' are unusual because they feature flap-down goggles made as part of the cap. Apart from
these examples, men's headwear was far simpler and plainer than the styles for ladies.*

This photograph illustrates how motoring clothing could make the wearer an object of fun. The rear passengers in this 1902 Argyll are dressed in ordinary woollen suits with caps but front passenger and driver have put on goggles and a dust coat and could only be motorists.

HATS, HOODS AND GOGGLES

'Dust is really the only drawback of automobile travelling, but it is a serious one, especially for women. The dust is overpowering; it fills one's eyes, ears, mouth and throat, and nothing seems able to resist it. The only real protection seems to be the unbecoming goggles and a hood to cover the head, made of some light material like light mackintosh. Even then the dust gets in at the back of the neck and into the hair. In France the women appear to wear very thick fur coats, small tight-fitting caps, thick veils, and spectacles. They have a glorious disregard for their personal appearance, as anyone must who really wishes to enjoy motoring. They come back in the evening buried in dust, and complain bitterly of the pain which they experience in endeavouring to wash the dust from their faces and eyes.' So wrote Lady Jeune in 1902, when protective headwear was crude and inelegant. Yet in the next few years motor millinery blossomed into many effective and stylish forms.

The Edwardian lady who wished to go motoring needed her hat and hair to be kept in order, the back of her neck and her ears to be shielded from draughts and her eyes protected from dust, winds and insects. These demands were answered by the hood and veil combination. Essentially hoods were large silk bags which completely enveloped the head. They slipped over the hat and covered the back of the neck and the sides of the head with sufficient length to be tied securely in a bow below the chin. Hoods gave the essential head cover and were spacious enough not to crush the hair. Most hoods were fitted with protection for the face in the form of mica or silicone 'windows'. These hood and mask combinations were amazing creations which resembled the headwear seen today in nuclear power stations. The windows were kept rigid by an aluminium frame and on the 'Buckingham' hood of 1906 the window could even be raised or lowered. Another example, the 'Lady Margaret' hood, had 'scientific ventilation' — three rows of holes punched all around the edge of the window. If the full facial screen was not desired then the lower half of the face could be covered in lace or gauze for breathing. Almost all hoods were made of silk but chamois leather with draw-string edges provided extra warmth.

An alternative to the claustrophobic hood and mask was the simple veil made of crêpe-de-chine, chiffon or gauze. Veils were recommended to be 6 feet 6 inches (2 metres) long and 2 feet 4 inches (70 cm) wide. They were pinned to the bonnet, pulled down over the ears and crossed behind the neck with the ends brought to the front to be tied into a bow under the chin. The colour of a veil was recommended to be a dust shade, so white, grey, navy blue and brown were preferred. Many veils were finished with white satin hems. The most dressy veils

Ladies' motoring hoods were amazing creations. Here the mica window can be raised or lowered and provided protection in summer from dust and draughts. These hoods kept the hair dust-free and neat, allowing for elegant presentation at the end of a drive.

RIGHT: *A mask of mica enclosed in an aluminium frame to keep its shape. Beneath this the lace veil is lined with chiffon to keep out dust and the side flaps are crossed at the back of the neck and tied in the front. The veil was made of silk and could be worn over any hat.*

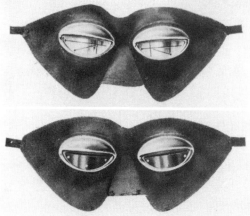

LEFT: *These goggles had metal eyepieces protruding from the top to give shade. The slits could be adjusted for individual vision requirements. The mask was made of waterproof material and priced at 6 shillings in 1911.*

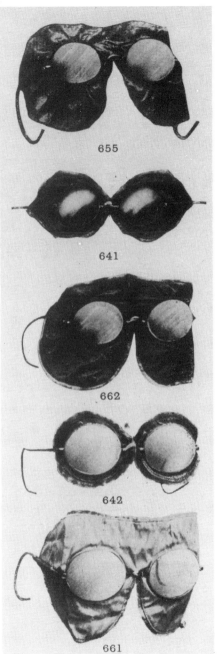

ABOVE: *In 1911 Dunhills offered this complete face mask, 'designed for ladies who wish to preserve their complexion'. It was made of leather and lined with white kid and sold for £1 1s.*

RIGHT: *All these goggles were made of silk, with glasses available in either clear or tinted form. They were edged with chenille fur for snugness and keeping out wind or dust. The nosepieces are all hinged.*

655

641

662

642

661

were of white, yellow, brown or navy lace and for extra strength were mounted on fine chiffon with elastic hems for a secure fit.

The choice of hat for motoring was bewilderingly varied. No one style was predominant for ladies. The general rule was that if the hat was to be worn alone it should be small, so offering the least wind resistance. With the security of a veil a larger style could be considered, but the motor car was no place for the very wide hat so common in the Edwardian era. Popular styles ranged from the Glengarry cap or the Tam o' Shanter to the straw bonnet or toque. No new design was specifically made for motoring but certain existing styles found popularity with motorists. If the hat was small, snug-fitting and warm then it was suitable, and motoring had some influence on the change in fashion from the wide-brim style to the smaller, close-fitting hat of 1912 onwards.

The choice of motoring headwear for men was usually the cloth or peaked cap so popular with yachtsmen. The cloth cap of tweed as worn for shooting, golf or fishing was considered perfectly suitable, and if flaps for the ears were fitted it was even warmer. The peaked cap was neater and rainproof and was a popular choice of King Edward VII when motoring. However, as the peaked cap became increasingly recognised as part of a chauffeur-servant's uniform the fashion for these caps among owner-drivers declined.

GOGGLES

Whatever the vagaries of motoring attire, there was one item which everyone agreed was essential: a pair of goggles. They were universally worn by men but women considered them far too ugly. More than any other item, goggles made motorists an object of ridicule to the general public. The cut and style of motoring clothes were generally elegant but goggles made the wearer seem laughable.

Basic goggles were made of thin convex glass surrounded by an edge of silk. There were enormous variations on this basic design, reflected in the 1902 Dunhill catalogue, which gave a choice of over thirty styles. Some had a metal frame with fine mesh on the sides for improved ventilation. A fur surround gave additional warmth in winter. Goggles were secured by either elastic straps or spectacle-type side bands to the ears. For added protection to the temples and cheeks, leather masks were available. The combination of mask and goggles was the most hideous of all protective clothing.

Leather gauntlet gloves were the most commonly used protection for hands and wrists. However, the Hand Protector allowed the driver to use his bare hands for steering. Made of leather and lined with fur, it must have been very warm and dry.

LEFT: *The 'Snuggery', a form of rug which enveloped the lower half of the body and was secured with straps at the back. It was lined with opossum fur and the outer skin was of leopard. This apron rug extended up to the chest and at the base there was a foot muff.*

RIGHT: *The foot muff apron of 1911 was the ideal answer for cold legs and feet. It was made in either wool or leather and lined with black lambskin fur.*

CLOTHING ACCESSORIES

After choosing a coat and hat motorists completed their wardrobe with a whole range of clothing accessories all designed for weather protection. There were gloves, boots, leggings, waistcoats, foot sacks and aprons.

Leather gauntlet gloves were almost universally used by men because they prevented the wind from getting up coat sleeves. Burberrys sold a garbardine gauntlet mitt with camel fleece lining. The palm was rubbered to withstand the wear and to obtain a better grip on the levers. There was a wrist strap for tighter fitting. Mittens were often preferred in cold weather because of the extra warmth gained by having all the fingers together

in one compartment. For the more eccentric, Dunhills made the Hand Protector, a sort of fur-lined leather bag that fitted to the steering wheel and into which the driver placed his hands.

Leather waistcoats were widely sold by motor clothing stores. One fine 1906 example was described thus: 'It is lined throughout with natural flannel, has silk sleeves and back, has wind cuffs, and as the leather is of the best, 21 shillings cannot be considered dear.' Used beneath a double-breasted tweed coat, for example, the leather waistcoat gave excellent protection from the cold for the chest.

The legs could be kept warm by wearing leather leggings or more suitably for ladies, high-legged cloth spats. Leggings were never truly becoming and by 1910 a motoring journalist complained: 'Of all the abominations for motor driving that persist I am of the opinion that what are known as gaiters or leggings are the worst.' Ordinary boots were often unsuitable for they kept the feet cold and damp. The answer, according to numerous advertisements, was overboots or foot muffs. Overboots were available fur-lined and of ankle or knee length. Gamages promoted an overboot of lynx and leopard or wolf and civet cat or dingo and leopard as the ideal Christmas gift. Many ladies did not like these boots because they made their feet look huge. The foot muff was just as bad and resembled a huge, furry backless slipper into which the shoe was slipped.

The motorist went to extraordinary lengths to keep his or her feet warm and dry. The foot sack was an example: the motorist would step into a leather sack and pull it up around the waist. In another version there was an open back with the apron lying across the lap and legs, and the feet went into a bag. The bases of these sacks had leather footsoles to assist the driver.

Driving the car while seated in a sack must have been difficult. Lady passengers favoured the sack because it prevented the wind from getting underneath their skirts. The leather sack or wrap-around apron had another useful and essential function. It solved the problem of passengers sitting in a pool of water that had accumulated in the seat after a storm. Alternatively ladies' leather motoring knickers with a detachable flannel lining could be purchased from Allweathers of London.

LEFT: *The leather waistcoat was widely used by all motorists well into the 1920s. It offered the ideal protection for the chest and arms against the cold and wind. It was made of specially dressed leather on chamois and lined with silk.*

BELOW: *Motoring attire at its most outrageous: a woeful-looking poodle in a leather coat, hood and goggles; Paris, 1903.*

24

A chauffeur in 'lancer' style uniform, with a double-breasted jacket buttoned high on to the shoulder. It would be made in melton or frieze and lined with tweed. The brown or black leather leggings were shaped to the leg. More expensive leggings were made of pigskin. The car is a 1912/13 Lanchester 38 horsepower.

CHAUFFEUR LIVERIES

'Nothing sets off a town car so much as neat liveries on the driver and footman, and, on the contrary, nothing detracts so much from the appearance of a car, no matter how expensive it looks, as a shabby driver' (*The Motor*, 1909).

The role of chauffeur was a natural progression from the coachman and footman of horse-drawn carriages. Some wealthy families changing over from carriage to motor car naturally expected it to be driven for them. In addition the workings of the motor car were a mystery and repairs were oily and dirty work. The chauffeur became both mechanic and driver.

For the ex-coachman turned chauffeur the wearing of livery was expected. However, if a mechanic was hired as chauffeur there could be difficulties. Fil-son Young wrote a book of guidance for the car owner in 1906: 'English mechanics are as a rule a good class of men, sober, competent and trustworthy; your only difficulty may be that some of them do not like being treated as domestic servants. That is to say, they may well object to wearing livery, and so forth. For touring work no one wishes to have his chauffeur in conspicuous livery; in fact nothing looks better than a plain, dark blue serge suit and peaked cap, which no one objects to wear.'

The chauffeur's outfit carried over many ideas from carriage days, for instance the neat, close-fitting double-breasted jacket with brass buttons and breeches. However, because of the higher speeds of motor cars the coachman's traditional top hat was replaced by the

RIGHT: *White or cream liveries were made of cotton drill for cooler summer wear. Some outfits had dark-coloured, detachable cuffs and collars for easier cleaning.*

BELOW: *A chauffeur stands beside a 1907 Daimler, wearing a double-breasted overcoat of plain design, available in melton or frieze and costing £5 5s. Overcoats were usually in the same style as the jacket and breeches.*

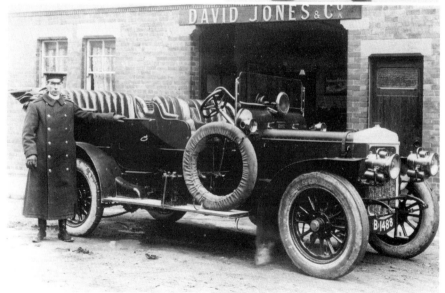

26

smaller peaked cap with a chin strap for security. Cap covers were also available in white for the summer and waterproof black. The peaked cap has remained the traditional chauffeur's hat.

Chauffeurs' suits were usually available in blue, green or grey. Leather suits were popular up to 1910 but soon became unnecessary for weather protection as improved car designs incorporated windscreens and high dashboards. Since leather never had the smart cut of cloth, leather suits soon became unfashionable. Cloth uniforms were made from melton, frieze or serge and lined with tweed. Tunics were double-breasted to the shoulder and fastened at the neck. Collars were wide and round. There was very little variation in the design of the tunics during the Edwardian era. The breeches and leggings remained part of the uniform long after they were necessary for open-car motoring.

From about 1910 a new uniform evolved as a result of the improved protection offered by cars and for more localised town driving. The new look consisted of double-breasted lounge jacket and trousers. The jacket was open at the neck to reveal a tie and shirt and had a wide collar and lapels. Some styles had piping around the edges of cuffs, pockets, collar and front.

By the late 1920s the popularity of enclosed saloon cars had finally caused breeches, leggings and boots to disappear from uniforms. The universal costume was now a lounge suit, white shirt, black tie, trousers and shoes — a uniform that has remained the traditional style for all chauffeurs.

This livery style has buttons only up to the chest. The leather gauntlet gloves have a knitted woollen wrist for a neater appearance. The leggings are in puttee style with straps to give a tighter fit. The car is an Albion 24/30 horsepower landaulette of about 1910.

The driver of this car in the 1903 Paris-Madrid race is the remarkable Madame Du Gast. She is wearing a double-breasted leather coat and gloves. The peaked soft cap has the flaps down around the ears and the essential face mask extends over the nose and cheeks.

MOTOR RACING COSTUME

Around 1900 major motor races were held on continental public roads. The cars speeding up to 90 mph (145 km/h) created a vast amount of dust. Seated high up on their huge machines, the drivers and mechanics were in a perpetual gale. So drivers, oblivious of what they looked like, wore the most hideous and monstrous outfits ever seen in motoring. Leather face masks, resembling death masks, were popular; goggles ranged from the standard glass eyepiece variety to the metal kind with three or four narrow slits. There were leather caps which fitted tightly to the head with flaps that came down over the ears to be secured under the chin. Later, aviators used the same style.

Protecting the head, ears and eyes from dust and wind were the main concerns of the pioneer racing driver. They were less concerned for the rest of their body. Any old warm clothing would do, usually overcoats, rollneck pullovers, corduroy or woollen trousers and stout boots. A driver and mechanic were expected to do all their own roadside repairs so rough working clothes were essential.

With the construction of concrete racing circuits, like Brooklands in 1907, the dust problem ceased to exist. However, goggles were not abandoned because the eyes still needed protection from the wind. Dressing for safety and protection from injury was neglected before the

ABOVE: *Motor racing before 1914 was a gruelling sport over atrocious roads for long hours in all weathers. This driver is wearing a rubber-proofed umbrella coat with a tightly fitting neck of elastic rubber. The coat was stormproof but no air could get in to ventilate the driver when hot.*

BELOW: *Winter racing in an open car (a 1905 Gregoire) with no front brakes seems madness. The driver is wearing a leather hood with the sides buttoned up in front of the chin. The full-length coat is rubber-proofed and probably the 'umbrella' variety.*

LEFT: *Frequently racing drivers wore rollneck jumpers and any old warm pair of trousers for easier movement. A chamois leather face mask resembles the balaclava worn by modern racing drivers. The goggles have protruding metal shades for protection against glaring sunlight.*

BELOW: *It must have been hot work changing the tyre of this 3 litre Vauxhall in these cumbersome leather coats and caps. The competitor (left) in this 1912 race is wearing two pairs of goggles for a rapid change when one set became dirty.*

Second World War. Drivers were not strapped into their cars and despite the risk of being thrown from the vehicle their heads were unprotected. Crash helmets were rarely worn before 1939, yet the racing driver and record breaker Sir Henry Segrave was one of the first to wear a helmet in the 1920s. In 1952 the FIA (Federation Internationale de l'Automobile), the world governing body of motor racing, made the wearing of crash helmets compulsory. The first helmets resembled upturned pudding basins and protected only the top of the skull. By the 1950s the standard design incorporated a peak and the helmet now extended over the temples and ears. Goggles were still mainly used. In the 1960s the full-face helmet was introduced to provide complete head and face protection. The visor allows greater visibility and is tough enough to withstand a blast from a twelve-bore shotgun. Racing helmets displayed the driver's individual colours for better identification. For ex-ample, Jackie Stewart's helmet was white with a Scottish tartan strip around it. The Grand Prix driver's helmet of today has a built-in radio for driver-pit communication, an oxygen supply tube in case of fumes from a fire and another tube to the mouth to provide liquid and prevent dehydration.

Protection from fire is the greatest concern for a Grand Prix racing driver as he sits low down between two tanks containing 48 gallons (220 litres) of fuel. Therefore every item of clothing is made from fire-resistant material — socks, underwear, gloves, balaclava and an overall suit. A quadruple layer suit made of Nomex will give protection for about a minute if set on fire. These thick suits also serve to display sponsors' names, which will be seen by millions of television viewers around the world.

Motor racing and rallying remain the last kinds of motoring that require specialised clothing.

The modern racing suit, as worn by Alain Prost, is made of Nomex fireproofed material. Up to four layers thick, it feels hot and bulky. Underneath, Nomex long johns and rollneck pullover are also worn. Sponsors buy space on the suit to display their names.

FURTHER READING

There is no other book exclusively on motoring fashion so for further study one must refer to the original regular reports in periodicals such as *Autocar, The Motor* and *Car Illustrated* (all up to 1914). General books on Edwardian life, sports clothes or motoring may also contain references to motoring costume.

PLACES TO VISIT

The following places each have a few items of motoring clothing, but other local museums may also have examples. Intending visitors are advised to find out the opening times before making a special journey.

Gallery of English Costume, Platt Hall, Platt Fields, Rusholme, Manchester M14 5LL. Telephone: 061-224 5217.

Gunnersbury Park Museum, Gunnersbury Park, London W3 8LQ. Telephone: 01-992 1612.

Hampshire County Museum Service, Chilcomb House, Chilcomb Lane, Bar End, Winchester, Hampshire SO23 8RD. Telephone: Winchester (0962) 66242.

Melrose Motor Museum, Annay Road, Melrose, Roxburghshire, Scotland TD6 9LW. Telephone: Melrose (089 682) 2624.

The Museum of Costume, Assembly Rooms, Alfred Street, Bath, Avon BA1 2QH. Telephone: Bath (0225) 61111 extension 327.

Museum of Costume and Textiles, 51 Castlegate, Nottingham NG1 6AF. Telephone: Nottingham (0602) 411881.

National Motor Museum, John Montagu Building, Beaulieu, Brockenhurst, Hampshire SO42 7ZN. Telephone: Beaulieu (0590) 612345.

The crash helmet became compulsory in top-class racing from 1952. The full-face helmet of today features a visor, all-round skull and face protection and inputs for oxygen and radio communication. Under the helmet a balaclava of fireproofed material is worn.